PRIME TIME FAMILY SERIES

DONNA ERICKSON'S
Year-Round Holiday
FUN BOOK

Illustrated by David LaRochelle

Augsburg
MINNEAPOLIS

8266991

To the memory of Great Aunt Ina,
who kept our family holiday traditions alive.

DONNA ERICKSON'S YEAR-ROUND HOLIDAY FUN BOOK

All previously unpublished material and all material originally published in *More Prime Time Activities with Kids* is copyright © Donna Erickson. All material originally published in *Prime Time Together . . . wth Kids* is copyright © Augsburg Fortress. All rights reserved. Except for brief quotations in critical articles or reviews, no part of this book may be reproduced in any manner without prior written permission from the publisher. Write to: Permissions, Augsburg Fortress, 426 S. Fifth St., Box 1209, Minneapolis, MN 55440.

Cover design by David Meyer
Cover photograph by Ann Marsden

Library of Congress Cataloging-in-Publication Data

Erickson, Donna
    Donna Erickson's year-round holiday fun book / by Donna Erickson ;
illustrated by David LaRochelle.
        p. cm. — (Prime time family series)
    ISBN 0-8066-2974-6 (alk. paper)
    1. Amusements. 2. Creative activities and seat work. 3. Family recreation.
4. Holidays—United States. I. Title. II. Series.
GV1203.E6737 1996
793'.01'922—dc20   96-19950
                                                                                          CIP

The paper used in this publication meets the minimum requirements of American National Standard for Information Sciences—Permanence of Paper for Printed Library Materials, ANSI Z329.48-1984.

∞

Manufactured in the U.S.A.   AF 9-2974

What's Inside

Notes from Donna

A Year of Holiday Fun

Welcome a new year of family life, with its unlimited possibilities of growing together and building memories! This book is all about diversions from routine that offer us a chance to celebrate. You'll find exciting ideas to enhance your family traditions as you prepare for major holidays, such as New Year's Day, Easter, Independence Day, Thanksgiving, and Christmas. You'll also find suggestions for turning quieter holidays and special days into wonderful celebrations and family learning experiences.

As families celebrate together, children develop a greater appreciation of the customs and values of the past, and an eagerness to preserve those traditions for the future.

Here are a few tips to make family celebrations even more enjoyable:

• Be an expert in holiday lightheartedness. Let loose and have fun. Sing holiday songs and dress up like holiday heroes. Tell silly stories and laugh at old jokes—even if you hear the same ones every day.

• Relax as you work with children on decorations and crafts. When you can't beat 'em, join 'em. Throw yourself into the spirit of playful celebration and see each event through kids' eyes.

• Keep imagination and curiosity alive. Not everything is as it seems. Think of the wonderful creatures created by the child's mind in all of us: leprechauns, talking bunnies, a red-nosed reindeer, and even toy-making elves.

• Bend the rules of routine—especially around holiday time. Ponder seasonal wonders, savor hugs, and say special bedtime prayers. These shared memories are the glue that keeps families together.

Here's to a year of great family holidays

Donna Erickson

5

New Year's Day

A New Year's Memory Party

You will need: slides, videos, or pictures of
                 family activities from the past year
            hot cocoa or hot apple cider
            popcorn snack

New Year's Day has not always been observed on the first of January. Long ago in Europe, people celebrated in April with the first warm breezes of spring. Many years ago, in what is now Florida, Native Americans welcomed the new year in summer, when corn was harvested. Today, Chinese people usually observe New Year's Day in February. And the Jewish New Year, *Rosh Hashanah,* falls in September. But no matter when the new year arrives, it is always marked by celebrations.

Instead of going out to celebrate your new year, plan a special stay-at-home party with your family. It's a great way to recall the best of times from the past year and to look forward to the next. For starters, make some hot cocoa or hot apple cider, and try this popcorn-nut munchie:

Popcorn snack

    ½ cup melted butter or margarine
    ½ cup honey
    3 quarts popped popcorn
    1 cup nuts

Combine melted butter or margarine and honey in a small saucepan; heat until well blended. Add chopped nuts. Pour over popcorn and mix well. Spread the mixture in a thin layer on a cookie sheet and bake in 350° oven for 12 minutes until crisp. Stir often to avoid burning.

Enjoy the treats while you view slides, videos, or photos you've taken over the past year. This reminds kids of the many activities in their lives that make them unique. If there was a death of a friend or relative during the year, take time to share memories of that person.

The party is also a great time to reminisce about funny and unforgettable moments. Encourage family members to reenact or retell a humorous situation and share their special memories.

You will need: sheet of thin cardboard
silver or gold foil
18" piece of red, white, and blue
  striped ribbon
small family photo
permanent black felt-tipped
  marker
scissors
glue

The third Monday in January is a national holiday honoring Baptist minister and civil rights leader Martin Luther King Jr. In your home, celebrate this important leader with activities that recall King's dreams and accomplishments for peace and justice in our nation and the world.

Make a Family Peace Prize. Martin Luther King Jr. was awarded the Nobel Peace Prize in 1964. Discuss with your family the ways conflicts might be resolved peacefully. Focus on specific world events or issues facing your community. Then talk about occasions when family members have tried to resolve conflicts calmly.

Encourage one another to demonstrate patience, self-control, and respect for others by creating your own Family Peace Prize. Design and then construct your family award together, using cardboard, foil, and ribbon. Print your family name across the front, and glue on a family picture.

On a regular basis, present the peace prize to the family member who makes real efforts to be caring and thoughtful to others.

Share a Dream. With your family, read selected portions of Martin Luther King Jr.'s famous "I Have a Dream" speech. (You can find the speech in your public library.) One by one, let family members share their dreams for a better world. For added impact, draw pictures to illustrate your dreams. Hang these on the wall or bulletin board as reminders to strive to live the dreams each day.

Valentine's Day

All-in-the-Family Valentines

You will need: 1 empty shoe box
1 small notepad and pencil on
    a string
festive valentine art supplies:
    doilies, crepe paper, hearts cut from
    construction paper, etc.
scissors
glue
tape

Take advantage of Valentine's Day and the week preceding it to build family relationships in a positive way.

This activity is a non-threatening vehicle for fostering communication and for sharing feelings that are sometimes hard to express eye-to-eye. You may even start a new family tradition with the valentine box!

Cut a 3" slot down the middle of the shoe box lid. Have the family decorate the lid and the box with colorful valentine materials. Place the lid on the box and tape the sides together. Tape the small notepad and pencil on a string to the top of the box.

One week before Valentine's Day, place the box on your dining room table. Encourage all family members and friends who stop by to pull a piece of paper off the notepad and jot down a special valentine note to each member of the family. (Older siblings or adults may help the younger ones with the writing.)

On Valentine's Day, gather for a special meal, then open the box and take turns reading the big stack of notes that have accumulated. Enthusiasm will have been building throughout the week, so expect your kids to be quite excited!

Have-a-Heart Munchies

You will need: large and small heart-shaped
cookie cutters
(for biscuits) biscuit dough
from your own recipe or a package,
bread board, rolling pin, strawberry
or raspberry jam
(for sandwiches) whole grain
bread, cream cheese, sliced tomatoes,
radishes, straw-berries
(for afternoon snack) apples,
cold cuts, cheese, crackers, cranberry
juice, and sparkling mineral water

Here are some easy-to-prepare, healthy foods that school-age children can make on their own and proudly serve to hungry family and friends as a special Valentine's Day treat. (Or Moms and Dads can tuck them into lunch boxes on Valentine's Day.)

Breakfast biscuits. Follow the directions for preparing your favorite biscuit recipe or use a purchased package of refrigerated biscuits. Roll out the dough on a flour-dusted bread board and cut out heart-shaped biscuits with the cookie cutters. Bake according to directions and serve hot with strawberry or raspberry jam. Or, place the biscuits and jam in a basket and serve them for breakfast in bed!

Noon sandwiches. Cut heart shapes from whole grain bread slices, using the larger cookie cutter. Spread cream cheese over each bread slice, and top with sliced tomatoes, radishes, or strawberries. Arrange on a platter and serve.

Afternoon snack. Use the small cookie cutter to cut cheese and cold cuts into heart shapes. Arrange with apple wedges on a plate and serve with crackers. Mix cranberry juice and sparkling mineral water for a snappy Valentine's Day beverage.

Birthdays

Fly a Birthday Flag

You will need: ½ yard heavy cotton or
                      canvas type fabric
                  scraps of cotton material for
                    letters and figures
                  fabric paint
                  fusible webbing
                  ½" dowel, 36" long
                  sewing machine
                  iron

Fly a personal birthday flag for your child to celebrate how special he or she is!

Cut a 24" x 18" rectangle from the heavy fabric and turn in a ¼" hem on all four sides. Sew down the hem with a zig-zag stitch. Fold ¾" of the left edge to the backside and sew down ½" from the folded edge. Check to see if the dowel fits snugly into the casing, then sew the casing closed at the top edge only.

Cut out the letters of the child's name from scrap material and, following the manufacturer's instructions, attach the letters to the flag with fusible webbing. Add additional designs to the flag to personalize it, using fabric scraps and paints. For example, if the child was born in the state of Colorado, add a border of mountains, or sew on a baseball and bat if the child plays on a team.

When decorated, hang the flag on your porch, from a tree, or inside your house on your child's birthday.

Party-Time Tips

• Let your child help plan the party. Choose a theme based on interests, favorite characters, or books.

• Young party planners can draw invitations that you can photocopy. Let the birthday child decorate them with markers and stickers.

• Have a get-acquainted activity as guests arrive, such as doing a simple craft, decorating cookies, or drawing pictures.

• Take instant snapshots of guests to send home for lasting memories, or tuck photos in each thank-you note your child sends.

• Jot down names of guests and events after the party is over. Package your review of the party along with cards for a special "memory box" your child will treasure.

St. Patrick's Day

The Growin' of the Green

You will need: kitchen sponge
grass seeds or alfalfa seeds
(available at health food stores
or co-ops)
scissors
plastic flower pot draining tray,
wide dish, or pie tin

After the long winter months, it feels good to see and smell fresh, green growing plants peeking out from the earth. Create that feeling indoors as you sprout your own shamrock for St. Patrick's Day.

If you want to see green growth in time for St. Patrick's Day, start your project at least a week early. Once your seeds sprout, enjoy the growing shamrock all month long.

Here's how:

With scissors, cut a new kitchen sponge into the shape of a shamrock.

Place the sponge on a plastic draining tray from a flower pot, a wide dish, or a pie tin. Generously sprinkle the shamrock sponge with grass seeds or alfalfa seeds.

Help your child distribute the seeds all over the shape. Pour some water into the pan. Keep the sponge moist, a perfect watering activity for preschool gardeners.

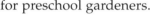

Once the seeds begin to sprout, place the shamrock in a sunny area of your home. Children enjoy taking a closer look at nature's surprises when they examine the sprouting seeds with a magnifying glass. Within a few days, the seeds will be growing, transforming a plain sponge into a beautiful green shamrock.

Place the shamrock on your kitchen table for a special centerpiece. For a party, you may enjoy decorating the shamrock with miniature toy figures or small St. Patrick's Day treats.

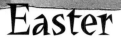

Easter

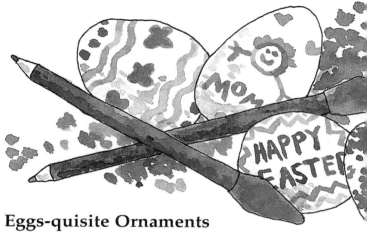

Eggs-quisite Ornaments

You will need: eggs
soapy water
darning needle
bowl
clear-drying glue (optional)

One traditional—and fun—way to prepare for Easter is by coloring eggs together. These decorating ideas are for use with blown eggs, which can be kept from year to year.

Wash the eggs in soapy water and dry them carefully. With a darning needle, poke a hole at each end of the egg. Twist the needle around inside the egg until the yolk is broken. Then blow hard through the hole on top. Collect the contents of the eggs in a bowl. Rinse out the eggshells and let them air-dry thoroughly before decorating. To strengthen the shells, coat them with clear-drying glue.

Sponged Eggs

You will need: several blown eggs
brown, green, blue
    tempera or acrylic paint
paper cups
small pieces of sponge,
    and spring-type
    clothespins (one for
    each paint color)
egg cups
newspaper
clear spray acrylic
    (optional)

Add a country touch to your Easter table with these easy-to-decorate eggs.

Working on a newspaper-covered surface, place egg in egg cup. Clip a piece of sponge to a clothespin and, using the clothespin as a handle, dip the sponge lightly into a paper cup partially filled with paint. Lightly dab the sponge over the top half of the egg. Let dry. Turn egg over and repeat for bottom half. When the paint has dried completely, an adult may spray the egg with clear acrylic for a permanent finish.

Crayon-Marbled Eggs

You will need: several blown eggs
glass jar (pint size or larger)
hot water
crayon stubs, peeled
vegetable grater
spoon
paper towels or newspaper
empty egg carton
clear spray acrylic

Decorate eggs with colored wax without having to heat the wax on the stove. Kids will marvel at the results!

Grate crayons over paper towels or newspaper. An adult should fill the jar with very hot (nearly boiling) water. Drop pinches of grated crayon into the water, and as soon as the wax begins to melt, add an egg, being careful not to spill water out of jar. Using a spoon, twirl egg in water. The wax will make a design on the shell. When you are satisfied with the design, carefully remove the egg and place it in a groove of an upside-down egg carton to dry. Experiment with different color combinations. Refill jar with clean hot water for each egg. When wax has dried, the adult may spray with clear acrylic to protect the design.

A Blooming Egg Tree

You will need: garden shears, hammer
vase or jar filled with water
decorated blown eggs

As the days begin to warm, take a nature walk with your children and look for young, budding branches. With garden shears, clip off branches that are about 20" long. Be sure to select branches that have large buds on them. Good choices are forsythia, lilac, tamarack, weeping willow, silver maple, and box elder. (If you are unable to find suitable branches, look for forsythia branches and pussy willows at your florist.)

Pound the clipped ends with a hammer. Bring them inside and arrange in a water-filled vase or jar. Place the jar in a warm room and watch for young leaves to begin appearing within several days. For fun, decorate the blooming branches by hanging blown Easter eggs on them.

A Special Sunrise

For a unique and meaningful experience, attend an outdoor sunrise worship service with your family on Easter morning. Look for locations and times in your newspaper. Enjoy a special breakfast when you return home.

A Hands-on Designer Shirt

You will need: fabric paint in several colors
sweatshirt or T-shirt in white
or light color
aluminum pie plate
waxed paper or cardboard

Kids of all ages will enjoy adding their personal touch to a gift that Mom, Dad, or a grandparent will wear proudly.

Lay the shirt flat on a work surface. Place a piece of waxed paper or cardboard between the two layers of fabric to protect the reverse side from any paint that may soak through. Mix paint and water (10 parts paint, 1 part water) in the pie plate. Place a child's hand (palm down) in the paint and guide the painted hand to the shirt. Gently but firmly press the hand on the shirt, making sure that the palm and five fingers make a print. Quickly lift the hand from the shirt. Allow handprint to dry and then repeat the procedure for each child's hand, using a different color of paint for each person.

If there is an unborn baby in the family, add a "baby's footprint" to the shirt too! Dip the side of a child's fist in paint and add five tiny toes with fingerprints of paint.

For other gift ideas, add handprints to pot holders, kitchen towels, or a sheet of paper that Mom or Dad can frame for the home or office.

Promise Gift Book

You will need: 6 pieces of typing paper, 2" x 5"
                 2 pieces of construction paper,
                   2" x 5"
                 felt-tipped markers
                 stapler and staples
                 regular letter size envelope
                 stickers (optional)

Make a booklet of coupons as a special gift for Mom or Dad.

Let the kids come up with six ideas for things they can do for the person receiving the gift, like completing some chore around the house, running an errand, baby-sitting a sibling, singing a song or giving a hug.

On each piece of paper, write the activity. For example: "This coupon is worth 10 minutes of playing ball with Andrew when Dad comes home" or "This coupon is worth one bike ride around the lake with Annie." Add decorations, and for fun write "No expiration date" on the bottom.

Staple the coupons together between two pieces of construction paper. On the cover, write a message suitable for the occasion, such as "Happy Mother's Day to the World's Best Mom!"

Decorate the coupon book and put it in an envelope and deliver it with a hug!

Memorial Day

Memorial Day Memory Trip

You will need: picnic lunch for the whole family

a pot or two of blooming flowers

How about setting aside the Saturday morning of Memorial Day weekend for a family trip into the past? Pile everyone into the car to visit the cemetery where family members are buried. Take along a picnic lunch and some flowers to plant on the grave sites of relatives.

Join your children on a ramble past graves of family members who have died recently or long ago, reminiscing as you read the names and dates. Then let your children place flowers at the grave sites.

Later, stop in a park (or, if possible, at a grassy spot overlooking the cemetery) and set out a picnic lunch. As you eat, talk about your family history and how departed relatives helped shape that history. Recall the red, white, and blue flags that dotted the cemetery and discuss the wars that those markers symbolize.

As you share family stories with your children, they will be drawn into that past to better claim the values and hopes bequeathed to them by generations of family members.

Death is one of those topics we often shy away from. Sometimes it takes the loss of a pet gerbil or goldfish, or the Memorial Day weekend, to bring it into focus— a reminder that each of us is part of something much bigger than the small world we stumble around in from day to day.

Independence Day

A Dot-to-Dot, Red, White, and Blue Pizza

You will need: one package of refrigerator
sugar-cookie dough (available
in grocery store dairy case)
8-ounce package of low-calorie
cream cheese (softened)
1 tablespoon milk
1 teaspoon shredded orange or
lemon peel
fresh blueberries and straw-
berries
round pizza pan
red, white, and blue birthday
candles

Your kids will enjoy helping with a Fourth of July lunch when you work together to prepare the dessert—an easy-to-make "pizza" in red, white, and blue.

Here's how to make a "dot-to-dot" fruit dessert pizza:

An adult should open one package of refrigerator sugar-cookie dough, available in the dairy case at your grocery store. Show your child how to press the dough into a round pizza-crust shape, on an ungreased pizza pan. An adult should bake the dough according to package instructions or until the edge of the dough is firm. Cool completely.

In a mixing bowl, stir together one 8-ounce package of low-calorie cream cheese (softened), 1 tablespoon of milk, and 1 teaspoon of shredded orange or lemon peel.

Spread the cream cheese mixture over the baked cookie dough. With a toothpick, an adult should poke holes in the cream cheese to make a large star pattern. Let your child place rinsed and dried fresh blueberries on the pattern in a dot-to-dot fashion. Fill in the star with sliced fresh strawberries.

Just before serving, poke red, white, and blue birthday candles in the fruit pizza. An adult should light the candles as family and friends sing a favorite patriotic song. The fruit pizza makes 16 small servings.

Back-to-School Day

Countdown to School

Here are ideas for veteran students and eager kindergartners ready to embark on a new school year.

School supplies. Whether they're touting school supplies, clothing, or backpacks, advertising campaigns are targeted to the back-to-school crowd every August. Collect the ads and prepare for a savvy shopping spree. Your kids can brush up on their math and writing skills as they count their money, compare prices, and make lists of needed clothing and school supplies.

Labeling. Pick up a permanent marker to label all of your kids' supplies and clothing before they take them to school.

Get ready for homework. Set aside a comfortable, quiet place where each child can do homework. It should be well lighted and free of distractions.

Care Pack for College Kids

If your child's baby-sitter or an older sibling is heading for college, send that person off with a surprise care package.

- A drawstring pouch filled with quarters for laundry machines and telephone calls home.
- A mug and packets of instant cocoa, soup, coffee, and tea.
- An adjustable reading lamp.
- Stationery and stamps.
- A photo collage of family members and friends.
- A small tool kit, including a hammer and screwdriver.
- A reliable alarm clock.

Calming the
Back-to-School Jitters

Remember your first day in a new school, or the day you started junior high? Were you worried about what the teachers would be like, about remembering your locker combination, about how big the big kids really were going to be?

New schools, new teachers and classmates, and anticipated homework all cause back-to-school butterflies. These can be especially worrisome when a child changes schools or moves into junior high or middle school. Here are some ideas to create a positive tone for your children's opening week of school—no matter what grade they are in.

• Listen to your child's concerns. Don't say he or she is wrong for having fears.

• Help your child think through alternative strategies for solving an anticipated problem. If opening lockers or forgetting the combinations is a fear, walk through a plan of action if the fear becomes a reality. For example, who should the child talk to if the combination is forgotten?

• Arrange a time for your child to talk to a young person who has "been there before." Be sure this person understands that the goal is to alleviate fears, not create new ones.

• Take advantage of open-house opportunities for new students. Time spent wandering the halls and meeting new teachers is valuable.

• Sleep is important. If your child is still on "vacation time," begin a school schedule as soon as possible.

• Listen intently to your child during the first weeks of school. Find time before bed to hear how the day went and offer encouragement through any rough new experiences.

• Most importantly, although many kids—especially junior high students—try to act cool and grown up, remember they are still children.

Labor Day

Windows on the World of Work

Labor Day can be a good time to remind your children that everyone works in one way or another—and that work is very important.

• Plan a special outing to your workplace with your kids. Show them around and have a snack or lunch together. Let the kids wear visitors' badges to make them feel official. If children are not allowed in your workplace during regular business hours, make arrangements for an after-hours tour.

• Familiarize your children with the work skills of your ancestors. Compile a list of relatives and interview them or gather information from your family tree.

• For preschoolers, make a booklet of pictures showing what you do each day. If you're an at-home parent, children should understand that caring for home and family is important work.

• Talk with your children about their interests and skills and how these may apply to a future vocation.

Grandparents Day

Read-Aloud Gifts

You will need: construction paper (such as the
kind that comes with new shirts)
1" x 1" copy of child's school photo
glue
colored felt-tipped markers
or stickers

Showing appreciation for Grandpa and Grandma is important any day of the year, but your kids might think it's extra special to show how much they care on the first Sunday after Labor Day, Grandparents Day.

If grandparents live far away, send a cassette or video recording of children reading a favorite story.

For grandparents close by, reading stories together is a great way to share time. Let Grandma or Grandpa read one story, then reverse roles and let the child read.

Children can make a special bookmark gift to remind grandparents of the pleasurable time they spent reading together.

Cut a strip of construction paper 1 ½" wide and 4" long. Glue a 1" x 1" copy of your child's school photo at the top of the bookmark. Write a message on the bottom half, such as "From your No. 1 Reader, with Love." Color the edges or decorate with stickers.

Halloween

Pumpkin Heads

You will need: pumpkin or gourd (one for each person)
permanent, felt-tipped marking pens
acrylic paints, paintbrushes
glue
straight pins
newspaper
"found" items (see below)

Try something new this Halloween and decorate your pumpkins instead of carving them. They will last longer, and your children can take a more active part in creating them—you don't have to worry about sharp knives!

Before you start to decorate, wash the pumpkins or gourds, and dry them thoroughly with a towel. Then let the children scout out the house for "found" items they can use in decorating: buttons, string, ribbon and bows, construction paper, shiny paper, stickers, hats, cotton balls, candy, sunglasses, doll accessories, medals, cardboard tubes, fabric scraps.

Place all the items collected on a newspaper-covered work surface. Give each child a pumpkin or gourd and let each draw features on it with felt-tipped markers, or paint them on with acrylic paint. Once the features are done, the real fun begins. Add hair, beards, accessories, by gluing items to the pumpkins or attaching them with straight pins.

Display the pumpkins or gourds on your porch, along a walkway, or perched on a tree branch, ready to catch the attention of October guests.

Great Costumes—Quick'n Easy

Putting together kids' Halloween costumes can be a last-minute ordeal. If you're scrambling to get your child ready for a costume party or trick-or-treating, here are some quick and easy tips that use readily available materials—and require *no sewing*!

• Start with old sweat suits as the base. Sweats are colorful, warm, inexpensive, and comfortable. With the addition of items from a jewelry box, an old attic trunk, or a neighborhood garage sale, you'll have one of a kind costumes. Kids can let their creativity run wild to develop costumes inspired by favorite book, movie, or TV characters.

• To turn your child into a Halloween Dalmatian, stencil various shapes and sizes of black spots all over a white sweat suit. Make a stencil by cutting out holes on a large index card. Use a sponge and black acrylic paint to dab on spots through the stencil. Also stencil spots on white tagboard cut to resemble ears. Glue the "ears" onto a headband.

• To make a cape for a king or princess costume, cut a piece of wide felt to the length suitable for your child. (Be sure it's short enough to prevent tripping.) Punch holes along the width with a hole punch. Weave heavy string or cording through the holes. Drape the gathered felt on your child's back and loosely tie the cording in front.

• Put reflective tape on all costumes if your kids will be outside in the dark. Neon dimensional fabric paints will also add a glow-in-the-dark effect when applied to clothing.

Thanksgiving

Thanksgiving Giving

You will need: a family commitment to share

By the time Thanksgiving vacation arrives, children are already talking about what they want for Christmas. Promotions, enticing ads, and conversations with friends begin to focus on "things" and the illusion of "having to have" coveted items. What a timely holiday Thanksgiving can be! When celebrated in its true meaning, Thanksgiving can change our focus. Taking time to thank God for what we already have and sharing our blessings with others can put us back on track in a hurry.

Thanksgiving is an ideal time to think about how you and your children can give to your community. Call a family meeting, and decide together what you would like to do. Your project may continue into December and culminate with Christmas. Or, better still, it can set a pattern for sharing that continues throughout the new year. Whatever the project, everyone—kids and grown-ups alike—will benefit from the experience.

Consider trying one of these projects:

- Collect food in your neighborhood and donate it to a local food shelf.
- Bake cookies or prepare a meal and deliver it to someone you know who is home-bound.
- Sort through closets and drawers for usable clothing that can be given to local relief agencies.
- Offer to baby-sit in December for parents with young children. This will give them a chance to begin Christmas shopping without kids in tow.
- Volunteer to run errands or grocery shop for neighbors who could use help.

Get Ready, Get Set . . .
Get the Whole Family Involved!

If your family is hosting a traditional Thanksgiving meal for family and friends, it's a big task to get everything ready. Here are ways to help make the festivities meaningful and relaxing for everyone—even the cooks.

• Get your kids involved in the preparations. They can make place cards for each guest and decorate them with markers, stickers, and nature finds, such as small pinecones, acorns, and leaves.

• When you're making a pie, children will enjoy rolling out leftover dough and using leaf-shaped cookie cutters or their fingers to create pie-dough leaves. Lay the shapes on an ungreased cookie sheet, sprinkle with sugar and cinnamon, and bake 8 to 10 minutes. When they've cooled, lay several of the leaves on baked pumpkin or pecan pies for decorations. Enjoy the rest as a snack.

• Teach older children how to prepare a traditional family recipe, such as cranberry sauce, pumpkin bread, or salad. The children may enjoy writing the recipe on index cards. They can decorate the reverse side of the cards with small pressed leaves or a crayon leaf-rubbing. Give the recipe cards to family and friends on Thanksgiving Day.

• Plan an outdoor activity, such as a "turkey bowl" football game for kids and adults to enjoy together before eating. Not only will the kitchen staff be free to tend to the meal uninterrupted, but the kids will let off steam and develop a hearty appetite.

Pilgrim Ship in a Nutshell

You will need: walnuts in the shell (enough
for each guest to have a half)
nutcracker
toothpicks
glue
white construction paper
white typing paper, cut into
2" x 2" squares
pen or pencil
scissors

Let the children help prepare for your Thanksgiving meal by making table favors from walnut shells.

Show the children how to crack the walnuts into halves. Pick out the nuts and set them aside for a holiday salad or the turkey stuffing.

Cut the construction paper into small 1 ½" triangular pieces and write the name of a guest or family member on each. Then thread a toothpick through each triangle "sail." Poke the toothpick into the center of a walnut-shell half. If the toothpick won't stand firmly in place, add a drop of glue. Make a boat for each person who will be dining with you. Place them beside the plates at your table.

As the guests arrive, give each person several small paper squares. Ask everyone to write short Thanksgiving statements showing appreciation for people present at the gathering ("I am thankful that Uncle Bob is so fun," etc.). Roll the papers into tight scrolls and place them in the appropriate boats. As the meal begins, have everyone at the table share the messages in their boats.

Hanukkah

Dreidel Decorations

You will need: 1 half-pint milk carton or a
small, square box
stapler
pencil, black marker
tempera paint in several colors
decorating materials: colored
tissue paper, foil, glitter,
fabric, scraps, etc.
glue

Hanukkah, the Jewish festival of lights, celebrates the rededication of the Jerusalem temple in 165 B.C. After recapturing Jerusalem from enemies, a man named Judas Maccabeus removed a pagan altar from the temple and led an 8-day celebration. Oil lamps were lit and, miraculously, burned all 8 days.

Dreidels are 4-sided toys that are spun like tops in Hanukkah games. You can create your own to use as a party favor, table decoration, or as a box to hold a small gift.

If you will use the dreidel as a gift box, place tissue paper inside the carton and tuck the gift in it. Staple the spout shut and paint the carton with tempera paints. When dry, turn it upside down and write a different Hebrew letter on each side. The letters look like this:

They begin the Hebrew words that translate, "A great miracle happened here."

Decorate the carton and poke the pencil through the bottom. If you are using a square box, poke the pencil all the way through and out the opposite end (see illustration).

Christmas

Family Holiday Hellos

You will need: 1 snapshot of each family
member doing something he
or she has enjoyed during the
past year
1 piece of 8 ½" x 11" white
construction paper
tape
white typing or printer paper
computer, typewriter, or
black pen

Here's a family Christmas letter that's fun to make *and* receive! Tape the snapshots to construction paper in a pleasing arrangement. If you wish, cut out the figures, trimming away backgrounds. Leave space under each picture for a short paragraph. Ask everyone to compose a few sentences about events of the past year. (If children are too young to write, let them dictate their thoughts in their own charming style.)

Use a computer, typewriter, or pen to put the words on paper. Include the name and age of each child and then tape the sentences near each picture. At the bottom, add your own comments and extend holiday wishes from the whole family. Let everyone sign— and add decorations, if you wish.

Take the completed project to be duplicated at a print shop. Prices vary according to the paper you choose and the quantity you order.

Wrap It Up—Together!

You will need: gift wrapping materials—
paper, ribbon, tape
items unique to persons receiving
the gifts

Here are idea starters for adding a special, personalized flair to gifts you wrap.

• If the gift is for a sports fan, wrap it in pages from a sports magazine and tie it up with a new headband.

• If a person enjoys gardening, wrap the gift with a floral fabric topped with seed packets tied into a bow.

• If someone loves to cook, print a recipe on the wrapping paper. Fill the package with ingredients in the recipe, and attach a kitchen utensil or gadget to the bow.

When you make a game out of gift wrapping, two hands might not be as easy as one!

Place the gift and wrapping supplies on a table. Stand next to a partner and work together to wrap the gift. Each person may use *only his or her outside hand*. (Keep the other hand behind you.) You'll discover how important verbal skills are as you team up to "wrap up."

Christmas Card
Maps and Memories

You will need: map of the U.S., North America,
       or the World
      Christmas cards and envelopes
       you have received
      scissors
      tape or thumb tacks

Whether you and your kids are brushing up on geography or learning map skills, here's an activity that's both fun and educational.

Post the map where it is seen readily. As holiday cards arrive, share the messages with your family and cut off the postmark from each envelope. Read the location printed on the postmark, locate it on your map, and tack or tape the postmark to the correct spot. If the location is not shown on the map, use the closest major city.

Don't forget to save the stamps—your kids can start a hobby that may last a lifetime.

During the days after Christmas, pause to reflect on greetings you received during the holiday. Sort through your cards and choose ones from relatives and friends. Distribute these to all family members. Then gather by the tree and take turns reading the greetings and any messages written in the cards. Kids especially enjoy hearing their names mentioned or news about cousins and friends who are their age.

Light Up Your Christmas

You will need: paper lunch bags
paper punch
sand
votive candles
antique blue or clear glass jars
    plain tin can with rough edges pinched
    flat and smooth
hammer
bath towel
nail
permanent black marker

Add a warm glow to holiday nights with these easy-to-make luminarias. Place the flickering lights along your walk, or on a porch to welcome guests. *(Note: adults should light the candles. Never leave children alone around burning candles.)*

Punched-Tin Luminarias. Fill a can with water and place it in a freezer. When the ice is solid, remove the can from freezer. Using a black marker, dot a design on the side (Christmas trees, stars, bells). Leave 1" from the bottom undecorated.

Place the can on its side on a towel. Punch out the design by driving a nail through each dot. (The ice prevents the nail from bending the tin.) Dump out the ice set a votive candle inside.

Paper-Bag Luminarias. Use a paper punch to create designs on the top half of the bag. Pour a cup of sand in each bag and place a votive candle in the center. Fold the top 1" of bag over and out to form a cuff.

Glass-Jar Luminarias. Place sand in the bottom of antique blue or clear canning jars. Nestle votive candles in the sand and tie a colorful ribbon around the jar.

Kwanzaa

Kwanzaa Treats to Eat

You will need: chunks of fresh mango, papaya,
pineapple, and banana
shredded coconut
skewers or long, round toothpicks

Kwanzaa, a week-long African American celebration, begins December 26. Kwanzaa, which means "first fruits," was created as a unique African American tradition that focuses on family and culture.

Each of the seven days of the celebration is devoted to one principle: unity, self-determination, collective work and responsibility, cooperative economics, purpose, creativity, and faith.

Kwanzaa is celebrated around the country with storytelling, poetry readings, dances and music, art exhibits, plays, and lectures. Share background about this holiday with your family. Stop by the library for some great children's books about Kwanzaa and read these together. Check your local newspaper for a listing of Kwanzaa events and attend some of them.

Many families top off the holiday week with a special Kwanzaa meal. Here is a delicious African fruit kabob you can serve as part of your celebration.

Poke chunks of fresh mango, papaya, pineapple, and bananas on a skewer or long toothpick. Arrange these on a platter and sprinkle coconut over the top. As you nibble on these treats, talk about the principles celebrated during Kwanzaa and the contributions African Americans have made to our nation.

Countdown to the New Year

You will need: cardboard tubes from bathroom
tissue or paper towels cut to
6" lengths
party favors—folded paper
party hats, key chains, whistles,
wrapped candy, etc.
strips of paper
wrapping paper, ribbon
pens, tape, scissors

Get ready for a great new beginning with a New Year's Eve celebration that involves the whole family.

New Year's Crackers. Here's an easy-to-make variation on English Christmas crackers—party favors that make a "cracking" sound when you open them. These are a silent version, but just as fun. Gather cardboard tubes and fill them with folded-paper party hats, whistles, wrapped candy, etc. Tuck in a strip of paper with a New Year's fortune written on it. Wrap each tube with festive paper. Twist the ends and tie with ribbons. Clip the ends to make fringe. Add name tags. Let everyone open the crackers at the same time and read their fortunes aloud.

Start the evening outside: Ice skating, hiking, sledding, flag football, capture the flag, etc. Then move indoors for a meal of soup, stew, or chili, along with salad and bread. After the meal try any of the following activities:

• Tell stories, sing songs, and play charades—let everyone act out "the most memorable event of the past year."

• Get out construction paper and pens, and write thank-you cards for Christmas gifts you received. For a special touch, add photos of each person playing with or using the gift.

• Take down the Christmas decorations. Make it a party by sharing holiday memories. If some decorations were garlands of popcorn, cranberries, etc., hang them outside on bushes for feathered friends. Add dry dinner rolls or bread to the feast. Roll pinecones in peanut butter and birdseed, and hang these from trees.

• Reflect on your responsibilities as members of the family and jot down resolutions for the coming year. Illustrate the resolutions and hang the pictures on the refrigerator as reminders of your goals.

Parents' Page

Timely Tips—Any Time of Year

Here are parenting suggestions that are appropriate for any time of the year, but especially during the extra hustle and bustle of holidays.

• Listen to what your kids have to say. Pay attention to stories, questions, worries, and wishes. Ask questions, repeat what you hear, seek clarification when you don't understand what they've said.

• Loosen up! Take time to play with your child. Parenting brings joy to your life.

• Try thinking of situations as challenges or opportunities rather than as something you can't handle.

• Take a minute to catch your breath and ease stress. Breathe deeply for 15 seconds whenever you feel overwhelmed. Prepare for potential stress by slowing down and talking through the situation.

• Praise your children for something each day. Encourage their efforts. Children live up—or down—to our expectations.

• As important as it is to spend time with your child, don't forget to set aside a little time for yourself—especially during busy or hectic days.

• Don't be afraid to ask for help. There are many people who can help support you in your parenting.

• Laugh at least once a day—it's okay to laugh at yourself!